Book 1

C Programming Success in a Day

BY SAM KEY

&

Book 2
PHP Programming Professional Made Easy

BY SAM KEY

Book 1

C Programming Success in a Day

BY SAM KEY

Beginners' Guide To Fast, Easy And Efficient Learning Of C Programming

Programming #14:C Programming Success in a Day & PHP Programming Professional Made Easy

Programming #14:C Programming Success in a Day & PHP Programming Professional Made Easy

Table Contents

Programming #14:C Programming Success in a Day & PHP Programming Professional Made Easy

Introduction

I want to thank you and congratulate you for purchasing the book, "C Programming Success in a Day – Beginners guide to fast, easy and efficient learning of Cc programming".

C. is one of the most popular and most used programming languages back then and today. Many expert developers have started with learning C in order to become knowledgeable in computer programming. In some grade schools and high schools, C programming is included on their curriculum.

If you are having doubts learning the language, do not. C is actually easy to learn. Compared to C++, C is much simpler and offer little. You do not need spend years to become a master of this language.

This book will tackle the basics when it comes to C. It will cover the basic functions you need in order to create programs that can produce output and accept input. Also, in the later chapters, you will learn how to make your program capable of simple thinking. And lastly, the last chapters will deal with teaching you how to create efficient programs with the help of loops.

Anyway, before you start programming using C, you need to get some things ready. First, you will need a compiler. A compiler is a program that will translate, compile, or convert your lines of code as an executable file. It means that, you will need a compiler for you to be able to run the program you have developed.

In case you are using this book as a supplementary source of information and you are taking a course of C, you might already have a compiler given to you by your instructor. If you are not, you can get one of the compilers that are available on the internet from MinGW.org.

You will also need a text editor. One of the best text editors you can use is Notepad++. It is free and can be downloadable from the internet. Also, it works well with MinGW's compiler.

In case you do not have time to configure or install those programs, you can go and get Microsoft's Visual C++ program. It contains all the things you need in order to practice developing programs using C or C++.

Programming #14:C Programming Success in a Day & PHP Programming Professional Made Easy

The content of this book was simplified in order for you to comprehend the ideas and practices in developing programs in C easily. Thanks again for purchasing this book. I hope you enjoy it!

Chapter 1: Hello World – the Basics

When coding a C program, you must start your code with the function 'main'. By the way, a function is a collection of action that aims to achieve one or more goals. For example, a vegetable peeler has one function, which is to remove a skin of a vegetable. The peeler is composed of parts (such as the blade and handle) that will aid you to perform its function. A C function is also composed of such components and they are the lines of codes within it.

Also, take note that in order to make your coding life easier, you will need to include some prebuilt headers or functions from your compiler.

To give you an idea on what C code looks like, check the sample below:

```
#include <stdio.h>

int main()

{

        printf( "Hello World!\n" );

        getchar();

        return 0;

}
```

As you can see in the first line, the code used the #include directive to include the stdio.h in the program. In this case, the stdio.h will provide you with access to functions such as printf and getchar.

Main Declaration

After that, the second line contains int main(). This line tells the compiler that there exist a function named main. The int in the line indicates that the function main will return an integer or number.

Curly Braces

The next line contains a curly brace. In C programming, curly braces indicate the start and end of a code block or a function. A code block is a series of codes joined together in a series. When a function is called by the program, all the line of codes inside it will be executed.

Printf()

The printf function, which follows the opening curly brace is the first line of code in your main function or code block. Like the function main, the printf also have a code block within it, which is already created and included since you included <stdio.h> in your program. The function of printf is to print text into your program's display window.

Beside printf is the value or text that you want to print. It should be enclosed in parentheses to abide standard practice. The value that the code want to print is Hello World!. To make sure that printf to recognize that you want to print a string and display the text properly, it should be enclosed inside double quotation marks.

By the way, in programming, a single character is called a character while a sequence of characters is called a string.

Escape Sequence

You might have noticed that the sentence is followed by a \n. In C, \n means new line. Since your program will have problems if you put a new line or press enter on the value of the printf, it is best to use its text equivalent or the escape sequence of the new line.

By the way, the most common escape sequences used in C are:

\t = tab

\f = new page

\r = carriage return

\b = backspace

\v = vertical tab

Semicolons

After the last parenthesis, a semicolon follows. And if you look closer, almost every line of code ends with it. The reasoning behind that is that the semicolon acts as an indicator that it is the end of the line of code or command. Without it, the compiler will think that the following lines are included in the printf function. And if that happens, you will get a syntax error.

Getchar()

Next is the getchar() function. Its purpose is to receive user input from the keyboard. Many programmers use it as a method on pausing a program and letting the program wait for the user to interact with it before it executes the next line of code. To make the program move through after the getchar() function, the user must press the enter key.

In the example, if you compile or run it without getchar(), the program will open the display or the console, display the text, and then immediately close. Without the break provided by the getchar() function, the computer will execute those commands instantaneously. And the program will open and close so fast that you will not be able to even see the Hello World text in the display.

Return Statement

The last line of code in the function is return o. The return statement is essential in function blocks. When the program reaches this part, the return statement will tell the program its value. Returning the o value will make the program interpret that the function or code block that was executed successfully.

And at the last line of the example is the closing curly brace. It signifies that the program has reached the end of the function.

Programming #14:C Programming Success in a Day & PHP Programming Professional Made Easy

It was not that not hard, was it? With that example alone, you can create simple programs that can display text. Play around with it a bit and familiarize yourself with C's basic syntax.

Chapter 2: Basic Input Output

After experimenting with what you learned in the previous chapter, you might have realized that it was not enough. It was boring. And just displaying what you typed in your program is a bit useless.

This time, this chapter will teach you how to create a program that can interact with the user. Check this code example:

```
#include <stdio.h>

int main()
{
        int number_container;
        printf( "Enter any number you want! " );
        scanf( "%d", &number_container );
        printf( "The number you entered is %d", number_container );
        getchar();
        return 0;
}
```

Variables

You might have noticed the int number_container part in the first line of the code block. int number_container is an example of variable declaration. To declare a variable in C, you must indicate the variable type first, and then the name of the variable name.

In the example, int was indicated as the variable or data type, which means the variable is an integer. There are other variable types in C such as float for

11

floating-point numbers, char for characters, etc. Alternatively, the name number_container was indicated as the variable's name or identifier.

Variables are used to hold values throughout the program and code blocks. The programmer can let them assign a value to it and retrieve its value when it is needed.

For example:

int number_container;

number_container = 3;

printf ("The variables value is %d", number_container);

In that example, the first line declared that the program should create an integer variable named number_container. The second line assigned a value to the variable. And the third line makes the program print the text together with the value of the variable. When executed, the program will display:

The variables value is 3

You might have noticed the %d on the printf line on the example. The %d part indicates that the next value that will be printed will be an integer. Also, the quotation on the printf ended after %d. Why is that?

In order to print the value of a variable, it must be indicated with the double quotes. If you place double quotes on the variables name, the compiler will treat it as a literal string. If you do this:

```
int number_container;

number_container = 3;

printf ( "The variables value is number_container" );
```

The program will display:

The variables value is number_container

By the way, you can also use %i as a replacement for %d.

Assigning a value to a variable is simple. Just like in the previous example, just indicate the name of variable, follow it with an equal sign, and declare its value.

When creating variables, you must make sure that each variable will have unique names. Also, the variables should never have the same name as functions. In addition, you can declare multiple variables in one line by using commas. Below is an example:

```
int first_variable, second_variable, third_variable;
```

Those three variables will be int type variables. And again, never forget to place a semicolon after your declaration.

When assigning a value or retrieving the value of a variable, make sure that you declare its existence first. If not, the compiler will return an error since it will try to access something that does not exist yet.

Scanf()

In the first example in this chapter, you might have noticed the scanf function. The scanf function is also included in the <stdio.h>. Its purpose is to retrieve text user input from the user.

After the program displays the 'Enter any number you want' text, it will proceed in retrieving a number from the user. The cursor will be appear after the text since the new line escape character was no included in the printf.

The cursor will just blink and wait for the user to enter any characters or numbers. To let the program get the number the user typed and let it proceed to the next line of code, he must press the Enter key. Once he does that, the program will display the text 'The number you entered is' and the value of the number the user inputted a while ago.

To make the scanf function work, you must indicate the data type it needs to receive and the location of the variable where the value that scanf will get will be stored. In the example:

scanf("%d", &number_container);

The first part "%d" indicates that the scanf function must retrieve an integer. On the other hand, the next part indicates the location of the variable. You must have noticed the ampersand placed in front of the variable's name. The ampersand retrieves the location of the variable and tells it to the function.

Unlike the typical variable value assignment, scanf needs the location of the variable instead of its name alone. Due to that, without the ampersand, the function will not work.

Programming #14:C Programming Success in a Day & PHP Programming Professional Made Easy

Math or Arithmetic Operators

Aside from simply giving number variables with values by typing a number, you can assign values by using math operators. In C, you can add, subtract, multiply, and divide numbers and assign the result to variables directly. For example:

int sum;

sum = 1 + 2;

If you print the value of sum, it will return a 3, which is the result of the addition of 1 and 2. By the way, the + sign is for addition, - for subtraction, * for multiplication, and / for division.

With the things you have learned as of now, you can create a simple calculator program. Below is an example code:

```c
#include <stdio.h>

int main()

{

        int first_addend, second_addend, sum;

        printf( "Enter the first addend! " );

        scanf( "%d", &first_addend );

        printf( "\nEnter the second addend! " );

        scanf( "%d", &second_addend );

        sum = first_addend + second_addend;

        printf( "The sum of the two numbers is %d", sum );

        getchar();

        return 0;

}
```

Chapter 3: Conditional Statements

The calculator program seems nice, is it not? However, the previous example limits you on creating programs that only uses one operation, which is a bit disappointing. Well, in this chapter, you can improve that program with the help of if or conditional statements. And of course, learning this will improve your overall programming skills. This is the part where you will be able to make your program 'think'.

'If' statements can allow you to create branches in your code blocks. Using them allows you to let the program think and perform specific functions or actions depending on certain variables and situations. Below is an example:

```
#include <stdio.h>

int main()
{
        int some_number;

        printf( "Welcome to Guess the Magic Number program. \n" );

        printf( "Guess the magic number to win. \n" );

        printf( "Type the magic number and press Enter: " );

        scanf( "%d", &some_number );

        if ( some_number == 3 ) {

                printf( "You guessed the right number! " );

        }

        getchar();

        return 0;

}
```

In the example, the if statement checked if the value of the variable some_number is equal to number 3. In case the user entered the number 3 on the program, the comparison between the variable some_number and three will return TRUE since the value of some_number 3 is true. Since the value that the if statement received was TRUE, then it will process the code block below it. And the result will be:

You guessed the right number!

If the user input a number other than three, the comparison will return a FALSE value. If that happens, the program will skip the code block in the if statement and proceed to the next line of code after the if statement's code block.

By the way, remember that you need to use the curly braces to enclosed the functions that you want to happen in case your if statement returns TRUE. Also, when inserting if statement, you do not need to place a semicolon after the if statement or its code block's closing curly brace. However, you will still need to place semicolons on the functions inside the code blocks of your if statements.

TRUE and FALSE

The if statement will always return TRUE if the condition is satisfied. For example, the condition in the if statement is 10 > 2. Since 10 is greater than 2, then it is true. On the other hand, the if statement will always return FALSE if the condition is not satisfied. For example, the condition in the if statement is 5 < 5. Since 5 is not less than 5, then the statement will return a FALSE.

Note that if statements only return two results: TRUE and FALSE. In computer programming, the number equivalent to TRUE is any nonzero number. In some cases, it is only the number 1. On the other hand, the number equivalent of FALSE is zero.

Operators

Also, if statements use comparison, Boolean, or relational and logical operators. Some of those operators are:

== – equal to

!= – not equal to

> – greater than

< – less than

>= – greater than or equal to

<= – less than or equal to

Else Statement

There will be times that you would want your program to do something else in case your if statement return FALSE. And that is what the else statement is for. Check the example below:

```
#include <stdio.h>

int main()

{

        int some_number;

        printf( "Welcome to Guess the Magic Number program. \n" );

        printf( "Guess the magic number to win. \n" );

        printf( "Type the magic number and press Enter: " );

        scanf( "%d", &some_number );
```

```
if ( some_number == 3 ) {

        printf( "You guessed the right number! " );

}

else {

        printf( "Sorry. That is the wrong number" );

}

getchar();

return 0;

}
```

If ever the if statement returns FALSE, the program will skip next to the else statement immediately. And since the if statement returns FALSE, it will immediately process the code block inside the else statement.

For example, if the number the user inputted on the program is 2, the if statement will return a FALSE. Due to that, the else statement will be processed, and the program will display:

Sorry. That is the wrong number

On the other hand, if the if statement returns TRUE, it will process the if statement's code block, but it will bypass all the succeeding else statements below it.

Else If

If you want more conditional checks on your program, you will need to take advantage of else if. Else if is a combination of the if and else statement. It will act like an else statement, but instead of letting the program execute the code block below it, it will perform another check as if it was an if statement. Below is an example:

```
#include <stdio.h>

int main()

{

      int some_number;
      printf( "Welcome to Guess the Magic Number program. \n" );
      printf( "Guess the magic number to win. \n" );
      printf( "Type the magic number and press Enter: " );
      scanf( "%d", &some_number );
      if ( some_number == 3 ) {
            printf( "You guessed the right number! " );
      }
      else if ( some_number > 3 ){
            printf( "Your guess is too high!" );
      }
      else {
            printf( "Your guess is too low!" );
      }
```

getchar();

return 0;

}

In case the if statement returns FALSE, the program will evaluate the else if statement. If it returns TRUE, it will execute its code block and ignore the following else statements. However, if it is FALSE, it will proceed on the last else statement, and execute its code block. And just like before, if the first if statement returns true, it will disregard the following else and else if statements.

In the example, if the user inputs 3, he will get the You guessed the right number message. If the user inputs 4 or higher, he will get the Your guess is too high message. And if he inputs any other number, he will get a Your guess is too low message since any number aside from 3 and 4 or higher is automatically lower than 3.

With the knowledge you have now, you can upgrade the example calculator program to handle different operations. Look at the example and study it:

```
#include <stdio.h>

int main()
{
        int first_number, second_number, result, operation;
        printf( "Enter the first number: " );
        scanf( "%d", &first_number );
        printf( "\nEnter the second number: " );
```

21

```
scanf( "%d", &second_number );

printf ( "What operation would you like to use? \n" );

printf ( "Enter 1 for addition. \n" );

printf ( "Enter 2 for subtraction. \n" );

printf ( "Enter 3 for multiplication. \n" );

printf ( "Enter 4 for division. \n" );

scanf( "%d", &operation );

if ( operation == 1 ) {

        result = first_number + second_number;

        printf( "The sum is %d", result );

}

else if ( operation == 2 ){

        result = first_number - second_number;

        printf( "The difference is %d", result );

}

else if ( operation == 3 ){

        result = first_number * second_number;

        printf( "The product is %d", result );

}

else if ( operation == 4 ){

        result = first_number / second_number;

        printf( "The quotient is %d", result );

}
```

```
else {

        printf( "You have entered an invalid choice." );

}

getchar();

return 0;

}
```

Chapter 4: Looping in C

The calculator's code is getting better, right? As of now, it is possible that you are thinking about the programs that you could create with the usage of the conditional statements.

However, as you might have noticed in the calculator program, it seems kind of painstaking to use. You get to only choose one operation every time you run the program. When the calculation ends, the program closes. And that can be very annoying and unproductive.

To solve that, you must create loops in the program. Loops are designed to let the program execute some of the functions inside its code blocks. It effectively eliminates the need to write some same line of codes. It saves the time of the programmer and it makes the program run more efficiently.

There are four different ways in creating a loop in C. In this chapter, two of the only used and simplest loop method will be discussed. To grasp the concept of looping faster, check the example below:

```
#include <stdio.h>

int main()

{
        int some_number;

        int guess_result;

        guess_result = 0;


        printf( "Welcome to Guess the Magic Number program. \n" );

        printf( "Guess the magic number to win. \n" );

        printf( "You have unlimited chances to guess the number. \n" );
```

```
while ( guess_result == 0 ) {


        printf( "Guess the magic number: " );

        scanf( "%d", &some_number );

        if ( some_number == 3 ) {

                printf( "You guessed the right number! \n" );

                guess_result = 1;

        }

        else if ( some_number > 3 ){

                printf( "Your guess is too high! \n" );

                guess_result = 0;

        }

        else {

                printf( "Your guess is too low! \n" );

                guess_result = 0;

        }

}

printf( "Thank you for playing. Press Enter to exit this program." );

getchar();

return 0;

}
```

25

Programming #14:C Programming Success in a Day & PHP Programming Professional Made Easy

While Loop

In this example, the while loop function was used. The while loop allows the program to execute the code block inside it as long as the condition is met or the argument in it returns TRUE. It is one of the simplest loop function in C. In the example, the condition that the while loop requires is that the guess_result variable should be equal to 0.

As you can see, in order to make sure that the while loop will start, the value of the guess_result variable was set to 0.

If you have not noticed it yet, you can actually nest code blocks within code blocks. In this case, the code block of the if and else statements were inside the code block of the while statement.

Anyway, every time the code reaches the end of the while statement and the guess_result variable is set to 0, it will repeat itself. And to make sure that the program or user experience getting stuck into an infinite loop, a safety measure was included.

In the example, the only way to escape the loop is to guess the magic number. If the if statement within the while code block was satisfied, its code block will run. In that code block, a line of code sets the variable guess_result's value to 1. This effectively prevent the while loop from running once more since the guess_result's value is not 0 anymore, which makes the statement return a FALSE.

Once that happens, the code block of the while loop and the code blocks inside it will be ignored. It will skip to the last printf line, which will display the end program message 'Thank you for playing. Press Enter to exit this program'.

For Loop

The for loop is one of the most handy looping function in C. And its main use is to perform repetitive commands on a set number of times. Below is an example of its use:

Programming #14:C Programming Success in a Day & PHP Programming Professional Made Easy

```c
#include <stdio.h>

int main()

{

        int some_number;

        int x;

        int y;


        printf( "Welcome to Guess the Magic Number program. \n" );

        printf( "Guess the magic number to win. \n" );

        printf( "You have only three chance of guessing. \n" );

        printf( "If you do not get the correct answer after guessing three times. \n"
        );

        printf( "This program will be terminated. \n" );


        for (x = 0; x < 3; x++) {

                y = 3 − x;

                printf( "The number of guesses that you have left is: %d", y );

                printf( "\nGuess the magic number: " );

                scanf( "%d", &some_number );

                if ( some_number == 3 ) {

                        printf( "You guessed the right number! \n" );

                        x = 4;

                }
```

```
        else if ( some_number > 3 ){

                printf( "Your guess is too high! \n " );

        }

        else {

                printf( "Your guess is too low! \n " );

        }

    }

    printf( "Press the Enter button to close this program. \n" );

    getchar();

    getchar();

    return 0;

}
```

The for statement's argument section or part requires three things. First, the initial value of the variable that will be used. In this case, the example declared that x = 0. Second, the condition. In the example, the for loop will run until x has a value lower than 3. Third, the variable update line. Every time the for loop loops, the variable update will be executed. In this case, the variable update that will be triggered is x++.

Increment and Decrement Operators

By the way, x++ is a variable assignment line. The x is the variable and the ++ is an increment operator. The function of an increment operator is to add 1 to the variable where it was placed. In this case, every time the program reads x++, the program will add 1 to the variable x. If x has a value of 10, the increment operator will change variable x's value to 11.

On the other hand, you can also use the decrement operator instead of the increment operator. The decrement operator is done by place -- next to a variable. Unlike the increment operator, the decrement subtracts 1 to its operand.

Just like the while loop, the for loop will run as long as its condition returns TRUE. However, the for loop has a built in safety measure and variable declaration. You do not need to declare the value needed for its condition outside the statement. And the safety measure to prevent infinite loop is the variable update. However, it does not mean that it will be automatically immune to infinite loops. Poor programming can lead to it. For example:

```
for (x = 1; x > 1; x++) {

        /* Insert Code Block Here */

}
```

In this example, the for loop will enter into an infinite loop unless a proper means of escape from the loop is coded inside its code block.

The structure of the for loop example is almost the same with while loop. The only difference is that the program is set to loop for only three times. In this case, it only allows the user to guess three times or until the value of variable x does not reach 3 or higher.

Every time the user guesses wrong, the value of x is incremented, which puts the loop closer in ending. However, in case the user guesses right, the code block of the if statement assigns a value higher than 3 to variable x in order to escape the loop and end the program.

Conclusion

Thank you again for purchasing this book!

I hope this book was able to help you to learn the basics of C programming. The next step is to learn the other looping methods, pointers, arrays, strings, command line arguments, recursion, and binary trees.

Finally, if you enjoyed this book, please take the time to share your thoughts and post a review on Amazon. We do our best to reach out to readers and provide the best value we can. Your positive review will help us achieve that. It'd be greatly appreciated!
Thank you and good luck!

Book 2

PHP Programming Professional Made Easy

BY SAM KEY

Expert PHP Programming Language Success in a Day for any Computer User!

Programming #14:C Programming Success in a Day & PHP Programming Professional Made Easy

Table of Contents

Programming #14:C Programming Success in a Day & PHP Programming Professional Made Easy

Introduction

I want to thank you and congratulate you for purchasing the book, "Professional PHP Programming Made Easy: Expert PHP Programming Language Success in a Day for any Computer User!"

This book contains proven steps and strategies on how to quickly transition from client side scripting to server side scripting using PHP.

The book contains a condensed version of all the topics you need to know about PHP as a beginner. To make it easier for you to understand the lessons, easy to do examples are included.

If you are familiar with programming, it will only take you an hour or two to master the basics of PHP. If you are new to programming, expect that you might take two to three days to get familiar with this great server scripting language.

Thanks again for purchasing this book, I hope you enjoy it!

Programming #14:C Programming Success in a Day & PHP Programming Professional Made Easy

Chapter 1: Setting Expectations and Preparation

PHP is a scripting language primarily used by web developers to create interactive and dynamic websites. This book will assume that you are already familiar with HTML and CSS. By the way, a little bit of XML experience is a plus.

This book will also assume that you have a good understanding and experience with JavaScript since most of the explanations and examples here will use references to that client side scripting language

To be honest, this will be like a reference book to PHP that contains bits of explanations. And since JavaScript is commonly treated as a prerequisite to learning PHP, it is expected that most web developers will experience no difficulty in shifting to using this server side scripting language.

However, if you have little knowledge of JavaScript or any other programming language, expect that you will have a steep learning curve if you use this book. Nevertheless, it does not mean that it is impossible to learn PHP without a solid background in programming or client side scripting. You just need to play more with the examples presented in this book to grasp the meaning and purpose of the lessons.

Anyway, unlike JavaScript or other programming languages, you cannot just test PHP codes in your computer. You will need a server to process it for you. There are three ways to do that:

1. Get a web hosting account. Most web hosting packages available on the web are PHP ready. All you need to do is code your script, save it as .php or .htm, upload it to your web directory, and access it.

2. Make your computer as simple web server. You can do that by installing a web server application in your computer. If your computer is running on Microsoft Windows, you can install XAMPP to make your computer act like a web server. Do not worry. Your computer will be safe since your XAMPP, by default, will make your computer only available to your use.

3. Use an online source code editor that can execute PHP codes. Take note that this will be a bit restricting since most of them only accept and execute PHP codes. It means that you will not be able to mix HTML, CSS, JavaScript, and PHP in one go. But if you are going to study the basics, which the lessons in this book are all about, it will be good enough.

Programming #14:C Programming Success in a Day & PHP Programming Professional Made Easy

Chapter 2: PHP Basics

This chapter will teach you the primary things that you need to know when starting to code PHP. It includes PHP's syntax rules, variables, constants, echo and print, operators, and superglobals.

Syntax

PHP code can be placed anywhere in an HTML document or it can be saved in a file with .php as its file extension. Just like JavaScript, you will need to enclose PHP code inside tags to separate it from HTML. The tag will tell browsers that all the lines inside it are PHP code.

PHP's opening tag is <?php and its closing tag is ?>. For example:

```
<!DOCTYPE html>
</html>
<head></head>
<body>
        <h1>Heading for the page</h2>
        <p>Some paragraph</p>
        <?php
                // Insert some PHP code in here.
        ?>
</body>
</html>
```

Echo and Print

PHP code blocks do not only return the values you requested from them, but you can also let it return HTML or text to the HTML file that invoked the PHP code blocks. To do that, you will need to use the echo or print command. Below are samples on how they can be used:

```
<?php
echo "Hello World!";
?>
<?php
print "Hello World!";
?>
```

Once the browser parses that part of the HTML, that small code will be processed on the server, and the server will send the value "Hello World" back to the client. Browsers handle echo and print values by placing them in the HTML file code. It will appear after the HTML element where the PHP code was inserted. For example:

```
<p>This is a paragraph.</p>
<?php
echo "Hello World!";
?>
```

<p>This is another paragraph.</p>
Once the browser parses those lines, this will be the result:
This is a paragraph.
Hello World!
This is another paragraph.
You can even echo HTML elements. For example:
<p>P1.</p>
```
<?php
print "<a href='http://www.google.com' >Google</a>";
?>
```
<p>P2.</p>
As you have witnessed, both echo and print have identical primary function, which is to send output to the browser. They have two differences however. Print can only handle one parameter while echo can handle multiple parameters. Another difference is that you can use print in expressions since it returns a value of 1 while you cannot use echo. Below is a demonstration of their differences:
```
<?php
echo "Hello World!", "How are you?";
?>
```
```
<?php
print "Hello World!", "How are you?";
?>
```
The echo code will be successfully sent to the client, but the print code will bring up a syntax error due to the unexpected comma (,) and the additional parameter or value after it. Though, if you want to use print with multiple parameters, you can concatenate the values of the parameters instead. String concatenation will be discussed later.
```
<?php
$x = 1 + print("test");
echo $x;
?>
```
```
<?php
$x = 1 + echo("test");
echo $x;
?>
```
The variable $x will have a value of 2 since the expression print("test") will return a value of 1. Also, even it is used as a value in an expression, the print command will still produce an output.
On the other hand, the echo version of the code will return a syntax error due to the unexpected appearance of echo in the expression.
Many web developers use the echo and print commands to provide dynamic web content for small and simple projects. In advanced projects, using return to send an array of variables that contain HTML content and displaying them using JavaScript or any client side scripting is a much better method.

Variables

Creating a variable in JavaScript requires you to declare it and use the keyword var. In PHP, you do not need to declare to create a variable. All you need to do is assign a value in a variable for it to be created. Also, variables in PHP always starts with a dollar sign ($).

```
<?php
$examplevariable = "Hello World!";
echo $examplevariable;
?>
```

There are rules to follow when creating a variable, which are similar to JavaScript's variable syntax.

> ➢ The variable's name or identifier must start with a dollar sign ($).

> ➢ An underscore or a letter must follow it.

> ➢ Placing a number or any symbol after the dollar sign instead will return a syntax error.

> ➢ The identifier must only contain letters, numbers, or underscores.

> ➢ Identifiers are case sensitive. The variable $x is treated differently from $X.

You can assign any type of data into a PHP variable. You can store strings, integers, floating numbers, and so on. If you have experienced coding using other programming languages, you might be thinking where you would need to declare the data type of the variable. You do not need to do that. PHP will handle that part for you. All you need to do is to assign the values in your variables.

Variable Scopes

Variables in PHP also change their scope, too, depending on the location where you created them.

Local

If you create a variable inside a function, it will be treated as a local variable. Unlike JavaScript, assigning a value to variable for the first time inside a function will not make them global due to way variables are created in PHP.

Global

If you want to create global variables, you can do it by creating a value outside your script's functions. Another method is to use the global keyword. The global keyword can let you create or access global variables inside a function. For example:

```php
<?php
function test() {
    global $x;
    $x = "Hello World!";
}
test();
echo $x;
?>
```

In the example above, the line global $x defined variable $x as a global variable. Because of that, the echo command outside the function was able to access $x without encountering an undefined variable error.

As mentioned a while ago, you can use the global keyword to access global variables inside functions. Below is an example:

```php
<?php
$x = "Hello Word!";
function test() {
    global $x;
    echo $x;
}
test();
?>
```

Just like before, the command echo will not encounter an error as long as the global keyword was used for the variable $x.

Another method you can use is to access your script's global values array, $GLOBALS. With $GLOBALS, you can create or access global values. Here is the previous example used once again, but with the $GLOBALS array used instead of the global keyword:

```php
<?php
function test() {
    $GLOBALS['x'] = "Hello World!";
}
test();
echo $x;
?>
```

Take note that when using $GLOBALS, you do not need the dollar sign when creating or accessing a variable.

Static

If you are not comfortable in using global variables just to keep the values that your functions use, you can opt to convert your local variables to static. Unlike local variables, static variables are not removed from the memory once the function that houses them ends. They will stay in the memory like global variables, but they will be only accessible on the functions they reside in. For example:

```php
<?php
function test() {
        static $y = 1;
        if (empty($y))
                {$y = 1;}
        echo $y . " ";
        $y += $y;
}
test();
test();
test();
test();
test();
?>
```

In the example, the variable $y's value is expected to grow double as the function is executed. With the help of static keyword, the existence and value of $y is kept in the script even if the function where it serves as a local variable was already executed.

As you can see, together with the declaration that the variable $y is static, the value of 1 was assigned to it. The assignment part in the declaration will only take effect during the first time the function was called and the static declaration was executed.

Superglobals

PHP has predefined global variables. They contain values that are commonly accessed, define, and manipulated in everyday server side data execution. Instead of manually capturing those values, PHP has placed them into its predefined superglobals to make the life of PHP programmers easier.

> **$GLOBALS**

> **$_SERVER**

> **$_REQUEST**

> **$_POST**

> **$_GET**

> **$_FILES**

> **$_ENV**

> **$_COOKIE**

> ## $_SESSION

SUPERGLOBALS HAVE CORE USES IN PHP SCRIPTING. YOU WILL BE MOSTLY
USING ONLY FIVE OF THESE SUPERGLOBALS IN YOUR EARLY DAYS IN CODING
PHP. THEY ARE: $GLOBALS, $_SERVER, $_REQUEST, $_POST, AND
$_GET.

Constants

Constants are data storage containers just like variables, but they have global
scope and can be assigned a value once. Also, the method of creating a constant is
much different than creating a variable. When creating constants, you will need
to use the define() construct. For example:
<?php
define(this_is_a_constant, "the value", false);
?>
The define() construct has three parameters: define(name of constant, value of
the constant, is case sensitive?). A valid constant name must start with a letter or
an underscore – you do not need to place a dollar sign ($) before it. Aside from
that, all other naming rules of variables apply to constants.
The third parameter requires a Boolean value. If the third parameter was given a
true argument, constants can be accessed regardless of their case or
capitalization. If set to false, its case will be strict. By default, it will be set to false.

Operators

By time, you must be already familiar with operators, so this book will only
refresh you about them. Fortunately, the usage of operators in JavaScript and
PHP is almost similar.

> Arithmetic: +, -, *, /, %, and **.

> Assignment: =, +=, -=, *=, /=, and %=.

> Comparison: ==, ===, !=, <>, !==, >, <, >=, and <=.

> Increment and Decrement: ++x, x++, --x, and x--.

> Logical: and, or, xor, &&, ||, and !.

> String: . and .=.

> Array: +, ==, ===, !=, <>, and !==.

Chapter 3: Flow Control

Flow control is needed when advancing or creating complex projects with any programming language. With them, you can control the blocks of statements that will be executed in your script or program. Most of the syntax and rules in the flow control constructs in PHP are almost similar to JavaScript, so you will not have a hard time learning to use them in your scripts.

Functions

Along the way, you will need to create functions for some of the frequently repeated procedures in your script. Creating functions in PHP is similar to JavaScript. The difference is that function names in PHP are not case sensitive. For example:

```php
<?php
function test($parameter = "no argument input") {
        print $parameter;
}
TEST("Success!");
tEsT();
?>
```

In JavaScript, calling a function using its name in different casing will cause an error. With PHP, you will encounter no problems or errors as long as the spelling of the name is correct.

Also, did you notice the variable assignment on the sample function's parameter? The value assigned to the parameter's purpose is to provide a default value to it when the function was called without any arguments being passed for the parameter.

In the example, the second invocation of the function test did not provide any arguments for the function to assign to the $parameter. Because of that, the value 'no argument input' was assigned to $parameter instead.

In JavaScript, providing a default value for a parameter without any value can be tricky and long depending on the number of parameters that will require default arguments or parameter values.

Of course, just like JavaScript, PHP functions also return values with the use of the return keyword.

If, Else, and Elseif Statements

PHP has the same if construct syntax as JavaScript. To create an if block, start by typing the if keyword, and then follow it with an expression to be evaluated inside parentheses. After that, place the statements for your if block inside curly braces. Below is an example:

```php
<?php
$color1 = "blue";
if ($color1 == "blue") {
        echo "The color is blue! Yay!";
```

```
}
?>
```

If you want your if statement to do something else if the condition returns a false, you can use else.

```php
<?php
$color1 = "blue";
if ($color1 == "blue") {
        echo "The color is blue! Yay!";
}
else {
        echo "The color is not blue, you liar!";
}
?>
```

In case you want to check for more conditions in your else statements, you can use elseif instead nesting an if statement inside else. For example:

```php
<?php
$color1 = "blue";
if ($color1 == "blue") {
        echo "The color is blue! Yay!";
}
else {
        if ($color == "green") {
                echo "Hmm. I like green, too. Yay!";
        }
        else {
                echo "The color is not blue, you liar!";
        }
}
?>
```

Is the same as:

```php
<?php
$color1 = "blue";
if ($color1 == "blue") {
        echo "The color is blue! Yay!";
}
elseif ($color == "green" {
        echo "Hmm. I like green, too. Yay!";}
else {
        echo "The color is not blue, you liar!";
}
?>
```

Using elseif is less messy and is easier to read.

Switch Statement

However, if you are going to check for multiple conditions for one expression or variable and place a lot of statements per condition satisfied, it is better to use switch than if statements. For example, the previous if statement is the same as:

```php
<?php
$color1 = "blue";
switch ($color1) {
        case "blue":
                echo "The color is blue! Yay!";
                break;
        case "green":
                echo "Hmm. I like green, too. Yay!";
                break;
        case default:
                echo "The color is not blue, you liar!";
}
?>
```

The keyword switch starts the switch statement. Besides it is the value or expression that you will test. It must be enclosed in parentheses.

Every case keyword entry must be accompanied with the value that you want to compare against the expression being tested. Each case statement can be translated as if <expression 1> is equal to <expression 2>, and then perform the statements below.

The break keyword is used to signal the script that the case block is over and the any following statements after it should not be done.

On the other hand, the default case will be executed when no case statements were satisfied by the expression being tested.

Chapter 4: Data Types – Part 1

PHP also has the same data types that you can create and use in other programming languages. Some of the data types in PHP have different ways of being created and assigned from the data types in JavaScript.

Strings

Any character or combination of characters placed in double or single quotes are considered strings in PHP. In PHP, you will deal with text a lot more often than other programming languages. PHP is used typically to handle data going from the client to the server and vice versa. Due to that, you must familiarize yourself with a few of the most common used string operators and methods.

Numbers

Integer

Integers are whole numbers without fractional components or values after the decimal value. When assigning or using integers in PHP, it is important that you do not place blanks and commas between them to denote or separate place values.

An integer value can be positive, negative or zero. In PHP, you can display integers in three forms: decimal (base 10), octal (base 8), or hexadecimal (base 16). To denote that a value is in hexadecimal form, always put the prefix 0x (zero-x) with the value (e.g., 0x1F, 0x4E244D, 0xFF11AA). On the other hand, to denote that a value is in octal form, put the prefix 0 (zero) with the value (e.g., 045, 065, and 0254).

If you echo or print an integer variable, its value will be automatically presented in its decimal form. In case that you want to show it in hexadecimal or octal you can use dechex() or decoct() respectively. For example:

```
<?php
echo dechex(255);
echo decoct(9);
?>
```

The first echo will return FF, which is 255 in decimal. The second echo will return 11, which is 9 in octal. As you might have noticed, the prefix 0x and 0 were not present in the result. The prefixes only apply when you write those two presentations of integers in your script.

On the other hand, you can use hexdec() to reformat a hexadecimal value to decimal and use octdec() to reformat an octal value to decimal.

You might think of converting hex to oct or vice versa. Unfortunately, PHP does not have constructs like hexoct() or octhex(). To perform that kind of operation, you will need to manually convert the integer to decimal first then convert it to hex or oct.

45

Float or Double

Floating numbers are real numbers (or approximations of real numbers). In other words, it can contain fractional decimal values.

Since integers are a subset of real numbers, integers are floating numbers. Just adding a decimal point and a zero to an integer in PHP will make PHP consider that the type of the variable that will store that value is float instead of integer.

Boolean

Boolean is composed of two values: True and False. In PHP, true and false are not case sensitive. Both values are used primarily in conditional statements, just like in JavaScript.

Also, false is equivalent to null, a blank string, and 0 while true is equivalent to any number except 0 or any string that contains at least one character.

NULL

This is a special value type. In case that a variable does not contain a value from any other data types, it will have a NULL value instead. For example, if you try to access a property from an object that has not been assigned a value yet, it will have a NULL value. By the way, you can assign NULL to variables, too.

Resource

RESOURCES IS A SPECIAL VARIABLE TYPE. THEY ONLY SERVE AS A REFERENCE TO EXTERNAL RESOURCE AND ARE ONLY CREATED BY SPECIAL FUNCTIONS. AN EXAMPLE OF A RESOURCE IS A DATABASE LINK.

Chapter 5: Data Types – Part 2

The data types explained in this chapter are essential to your PHP programming life. In other programming languages, you can live without this data types. However, in PHP, you will encounter them most of the time, especially if you will start to learn and use databases on your scripts.

ARRAYS

Arrays are data containers for multiple values. You can store numbers, strings, and even arrays in an array. Array in PHP is a tad different in JavaScript, so it will be discussed in detail in this book.

There are three types of array in PHP: indexed, associative, and multidimensional.

Indexed Arrays

Indexed array is the simplest form of arrays in PHP. For those people who are having a hard time understanding arrays, think of an array as a numbered list that starts with zero. To create or assign values to an array, you must use the construct array(). For example:

```php
<?php
$examplearray = array(1, 2, "three");
?>
```

To call values inside an array, you must call them using their respective indices. For example:

```php
<?php
$examplearray = array(1, 2, "three");
echo $examplearray[0];
echo $examplearray['2'];
?>
```

The first echo will reply with 1 and the second echo will reply three. As you can see, in indexed arrays, you can call values with just a number or a number inside quotes. When dealing with indexed arrays, it is best that you use the first method. Since the number 1 was the first value to be assigned to the array, index 0 was assigned to it. The index number of the values in an array increment by 1. So, the index numbers of the values 2 and three are 1 and 2 respectively.

Associative Arrays

The biggest difference between associative arrays and indexed arrays is that you can define the index keys of the values in associative arrays. The variable $GLOBALS is one of the best example of associative arrays in PHP. To create an associative array, follow the example:

```php
<?php
$examplearray = array("index0" => "John", 2 => "Marci");
echo $examplearray["index0"];
echo $examplearray[2];
```

?>
The first echo will return John and the second echo will return Marci. Take note that if you use associative array, the values will not have indexed numbers.

Multidimensional Arrays

Multidimensional arrays can store values, indexed arrays, and associative arrays. If you create an array in your script, the $GLOBALS variable will become a multidimensional array. You can insert indexed or associative arrays in multidimensional arrays. However, take note that the same rules apply to their index keys. To create one, follow the example below:

```php
<?php
$examplearray = array(array("test1", 1, 2), array("test2" => 3, "test3" => 4), array("test4", 5, 6));
echo $examplearray[1]["test2"];
echo $examplearray[1][1];
echo $examplearray[2][0];
?>
```

As you can see, creating multidimensional arrays is just like nesting arrays on its value. Calling values from multidimensional is simple.

If a value was assigned, it can be called like a regular array value using its index key. If a value was paired with a named key, it can be called by its name. If an array was assigned, you can call the value inside it by calling the index key of the array first, and then the index key of the value inside it.

In the example, the third echo called the array in index 2 and accessed the value located on its 0 index. Hence, it returned test4.

Objects

Objects are like small programs inside your script. You can assign variables within them called properties. You can also assign functions within them called methods.

Creating and using objects can make you save hundreds of lines of code, especially if you have some bundle of codes that you need to use repeatedly on your scripts. To be on the safe side, the advantages of using objects depend on the situation and your preferences.

Debates about using objects in their scripts (object oriented programming) or using functions (procedural programming) instead have been going on forever. It is up to you if you will revolve your programs around objects or not.

Nevertheless, to create objects, you must create a class for them first. Below is an example on how to create a class in PHP.

```php
<?php
class Posts {
        function getPost() {
                $this->post1 = "Post Number 1.";
        }
        var $post2 = "Post Number 2.";
```

```
}

$test = new Posts();
echo $test->post2;
$test->getPost();
echo $test->post1;
?>
```

In this example, a new class was created using the class keyword. The name of the class being created is Posts. In class declarations, you can create functions that will be methods for the objects under the class. And you can create variables that will be properties for the subjects under the class.

First, a function was declared. If the function was called, it will create a property for an object under the Posts class called post1. Also, a value was assigned to it. You might have noticed the $this part in the declaration inside the function. The $this variable represents the object that owns the function being declared.

Besides it is a dash and a chevron (->). Some programmers informally call it as the instance operator. This operator allows access to the instances (methods and properties) of an object. In the statement, the script is accessing the post1 property inside the $this object, which is the object that owns the function. After accessing the property, the statement assigned a value to it.

Aside from the function or method declaration, the script created a property called post2, which is a variable owned by the Posts class. To declare one, you need to use the keyword var (much like in JavaScript). After this statement, the class declaration ends.

The next statement contains the variable assignment, $test = new Posts(). Technically, that means that the variable $test will become a new object under the Posts class. All the methods and properties that was declared inside the Posts() class declaration will be given to it.

To test if the $test class became a container for a Posts object, the script accessed the property post2 from $test and then echoed it to produce an output. The echo will return , 'Post number 2.'. Indeed, the $test variable is already an object under the Posts class.

What if you call and print the property post1 from the variable $test? It will not return anything since it has not been created or initialized yet. To make it available, you need to invoke the getPost() method of $test. Once you do, you will be able to access the property post1.

And that is just the tip of the iceberg. You will be working more on objects on advanced PHP projects.

Conclusion

Thank you again for purchasing this book!

I hope this book was able to help you to learn PHP fast.

The next step is to:

Learn the other superglobals

Learn from handling in HTML, JavaScript, and PHP

Learn using MySQL

Finally, if you enjoyed this book, please take the time to share your thoughts and post a review on Amazon. We do our best to reach out to readers and provide the best value we can. Your positive review will help us achieve that. It'd be greatly appreciated!

Thank you and good luck!

Check Out My Other Books

Below you'll find some of my other popular books that are popular on Amazon and Kindle as well. Simply click on the links below to check them out. Alternatively, you can visit my author page on Amazon to see other work done by me.

Click here to check out Android Programming in a Day on Amazon.

Click here to check out Python Programming in a Day on Amazon.

Click here to check out C Programming Success in a Day on Amazon.

Click here to check out CSS Programming Professional Made Easy on Amazon.

Click here to check out C Programming Professional Made Easy on Amazon.

Click here to check out JavaScript Programming Made Easy on Amazon

Click here to check out Windows 8 Tips for Beginners on Amazon.

Click here to check out Windows 8 Tips for Beginners on Amazon.

Click here to check out HTML Professional Programming Made Easy on Amazon

Click here to check out C ++ Programming Success in a Day on Amazon

Click here to check out the rest of Android Programming in a Day on Amazon.

Click here to check out the rest of Python Programming in a Day on Amazon.

Click here to check out PHP Programming Professional Made Easy on Amazon.

If the links do not work, for whatever reason, you can simply search for these titles on the Amazon website to find them.